Miss Muffett and the Spider

Written by Deborah Eaton

Illustrated by Dennis Hockerman

Little Miss Muffet sat on a tire, eating her curds
and whey.

Along came a spider who sat down beside her
and frightened Miss Muffet away.

"That's it," said Miss Muffet. "First he sits on my tuffet. Now he is on my tire. I have to get rid of that pest of a spider."

Miss Muffet saw a girl. "Excuse me," she said.
"Can you help me get rid of a pest of a spider?"

"Sorry," the girl said. "I have to get to
Grandma's house." And she ran away.

Next Miss Muffet saw a frog. "Excuse me, sir," she said. "Can you help me get rid of a pest of a spider?"

"Sorry," the frog said. "I'm looking for a
princess to kiss, not a spider." And he hopped
away.

Just then, Miss Muffet saw a wolf by the fir tree. He looked big and bad. He had long fur.

"Excuse me, sir," she said. "Can you help me get rid of a pest of a spider?"

"No way," said the wolf. "I'm hungry and
thirsty." So Miss Muffet got out of there—fast!

Poor Miss Muffet ran right into a giant.

She tugged on his shirt. "Excuse me, sir," she said. "Can you help me get rid of a pest of a spider? He's sitting on my tire."

"Spiders aren't really pests you know," said the giant. "But okay. Fee-fi-fo-fum-fooooo!" And he blew the spider away.

Then—SPLAT!—he sat down on Miss Muffet's
tire himself.

"Excuse me," said Little Miss Muffet. "Can you
help me get rid of a pest of a giant?"